YAHRZEIT

YAHRZEIT

ALEX POCH-GOLDIN

Yahrzeit
first published 2005 by
Scirocco Drama
An imprint of J. Gordon Shillingford Publishing Inc.
© 2005 Alex Poch-Goldin

Scirocco Drama Editor: Glenda MacFarlane
Cover design by Terry Gallagher/Doowah Design Inc.
Author photo by Tim Leyes
Printed and bound in Canada

We acknowledge the financial support of the Manitoba Arts Council, The Canada
Council for the Arts and the Government of Canada through the Book Publishing
Industry Development Program (BPIDP) for our publishing program.

Canadian Cataloguing in Publication Data

Poch-Goldin, Alex
    Yahrzeit/Alex Poch-Goldin.

A play.
ISBN 0-920486-81-9

    I. Title.

PS8581.O15Y33 2005   C812'.6   C2005-903030-5

J. Gordon Shillingford Publishing
P.O. Box 86, RPO Corydon Avenue, Winnipeg, MB Canada R3M 3S3

For Hymie and Kathryn

Time will cease, peace will come
When the lion lays down with the lamb

Alex Poch-Goldin

Alex was born in Montreal and now lives in Toronto as a writer and actor. His play *This Hotel* was nominated for a 2001 Dora Award for Best New Play and was published by Scirocco Drama in 2002. That play was translated into French by Manon St. Jules, produced by Theatre la Catapulte and won the Le Droit/Radio Canada prize for best French language production in Ottawa. His play *Jim and Shorty* played at the Factory Theatre in Toronto and was later filmed for Bravo Television. A radio drama, *The Death of Simon Pinchuk*, was recently recorded for CBC Radio. His new play *Cringeworthy* will open at Theatre Passe Muraille in 2006 in a co-production with his company Planet 88. Alex has also written librettos for two operas, *The Shadow* and *Lisa*, composed by Omar Daniel. Alex was Playwright-in-Residence at Theatre Passe Muraille and was a member of the Tarragon Theatre Playwright's Unit. He is currently developing two new works, *The Life of Jude* and *Internazionale*.

Yahrzeit won the 2002 Toronto Jewish Playwrighting Award, has been translated into German, and will tour Germany, Austria and Switzerland in 2006.

Acknowledgements

Special Thanks: Kelly Thornton, Per Lauke, Marty Bragg

The Workshoppers: Paul Soles, Alison Sealy-Smith, Alon Nashman, Tom Rooney, Lucy Filipino, Quincy Bullen, Richard Greenblatt, Niki Landau, Kevin Hanchard, Sarah Orenstein, Rick Waugh, Jerry Franken, Dragana Varagic, Diane Flacks, and Dav Mickelson.

Also thanks to: Esther Arbeid, The Toronto Jewish Community Centre, Bonnie Green, Dave Carley, Glenda MacFarlane, Gord Shillingford, Hymie Poch, Velma Poch, Lawrence and Esther Poch.

All the Poches past and present.

In loving memory of Sonya Katznelson, Dave and Annie Medicoff, Rubie and Brenda Nelson and anyone and everyone mistakenly forgotten.

Yahrzeit was originally commissioned by CanStage in Toronto.

Dramaturged by Iris Turcott. German translation by Gerda Poschmann-Reichenau.

Playwright's Note

The character of Devon was written as a thirteen year old boy but for touring purposes was changed to an eighteen year old mentally handicapped character. Either version will work in the play, however a line cut in Act Two must be instituted if Devon is thirteen. "Look at the mental kid in my building. He's got plenty to worry about and he's happy." Also if Devon is thirteen the bowling shirt he receives should be too big instead of too small. The name Buhbzu is a term of endearment.

Characters

If the character of Devon is played as 18 years old, then he is developmentally challenged and has the intelligence of a boy about ten years old. When he speaks, his disability is apparent. He may also move in a physically awkward way.

Locations

Outside Meyer's apartment

Meyer's apartment

A Hospital Room

Time

The Present

Prologue

A spot light on DEVON drawing a chalk picture of a man on the outside wall of an apartment building—studied and intense. Lights reveal MARK standing behind him at the doorway of the building unnoticed, assessing the picture. MARK turns and enters the building.

Fade.

Scene 1

MEYER's apartment. MEYER's right hand is clenched in a fist as a result of his stroke. A Yahrzeit memorial candle is always burning in the corner of the room. There is a large oil painting on the wall.

MARK: Why are you limping?

MEYER: I got an ingrown toenail. It's killing me. If it gets infected, I could lose a foot. The clipper's in the drawer. *(He sits.)*

MARK: You put up my painting.

MEYER: I got a hole in the wall. Take a look at my toe.

MARK goes to get the clipper, stops and looks at an envelope on the table.

You didn't come yesterday, I sat all day.

MARK: What's this?

MEYER: What?

MARK: The Jewish Agricultural Fund?

MEYER: Ah, they want money for trees.

MARK: Trees?

> *MARK gets the clipper, sits down and takes off MEYER's slipper and sock.*

MEYER: In Israel. I bought trees when your mother died, now every month they send a form.

MARK: I don't want you buying trees in Israel. *(He attends to the toe.)*

MEYER: Why not?

MARK: Because of what's going on there.

MEYER: There's Jews there, they need trees.

MARK: How do you know what they use the money for?

MEYER: They're gonna send me a picture.

MARK: They could send everyone the same picture.

MEYER: You're paranoid.

MARK: You really got it wedged in.

MEYER: It's killing me.

MARK: And what if they cut down the trees to build settlements? Or divert the funds to the military.

MEYER: It's for pleasure. To sit in the shade.

MARK: You have no idea what's going on there.

MEYER: They're fighting Arabs, what else is new.

MARK: Look at the misery. You want to support that? Tell me if this hurts.

MEYER: So the bombers keep coming, it all balances out. Ah!

MARK: Wonderful, a perpetual state of mutual hatred. If they'd give back the territories there'd be a Palestinian state and that would be that.

MEYER: And if the Arabs had a state, there wouldn't be a war? With the airport and the ships, they wouldn't bring in weapons?

MARK: Well, if Israelis are killing innocent people…

MEYER: Innocent! Markie, they teach anti-Semitism at the schools. It's in their bones. Read the *Canadian Jewish News*. Ow!

MARK: If they had something to live for they'd stop killing Jews. Pass me a Kleenex.

MEYER: It's bleeding?

MARK: Yah.

MEYER: And before Israel existed the Grand Mufti of Jerusalem wasn't a Nazi? He sided with Hitler against us. I remember. They'll never be satisfied 'til the Jews are gone. That's that.

MARK: If it wasn't for Hitler there wouldn't be a Jewish State.

MEYER: So send him a thank you card. *(Beat.)* One thing I know, it's good Israel's there.

MARK: Despots of the Middle East.

MEYER: You teach geography, what do you know from politics. Did you get it?

MARK: You shouldn't pick.

MEYER: I don't pick. We Jacobs all have bad feet. Your toes are all too short.

MARK: No they're not.

MEYER: Show me.

MARK: What?

MEYER: Show me your foot, you don't speak English?

          MARK takes off his sock and shoe.

MARK: See, they're normal.

MEYER: That one's warped.

MARK: I broke that playing baseball.

MEYER: It was always deformed.

MARK: What are you talking about, I broke that toe.

MEYER: On the other foot you broke that toe. *(Beat.)*

MARK: Oh ya.

MEYER: The Jacobs all have ugly feet.

MARK: OK, keep still.

MEYER: Aie aie aie! You trying to murder me?

MARK: Hang on. There.

MEYER: Danken Got. *(Thank God.)*

MARK: Don't pick any more.

MEYER: Who picks?

        MARK puts on his sock and shoe.

        How's Carol?

MARK: Good.

MEYER: Is she pregnant yet?

MARK: She has a big case coming up.

MEYER: So.

MARK: So nothing. She's busy.

MEYER: What's the matter. You got a problem?

MARK: What?

MEYER: If you don't stick it in, it doesn't work.

MARK: I know, thanks. Two hundred is enough?

MEYER: I'm an old man already, you wait any longer, I'll be in a box.

MARK starts to write a cheque.

MARK: Dad. *(Beat.)*

MEYER: I got a new medicine I got to get. And light bulbs.

MARK: Three?

MEYER: Sure.

MARK: OK. *(He hands him the cheque.)* How's the therapy?

MEYER: What?

MARK: Your hand.

MEYER: It's fine.

MARK: You had a stroke.

MEYER: I got another hand.

MARK: I paid for this.

MEYER: To sit with a bunch of old people squeezing a ball?

MARK: Menkes goes to therapy.

MEYER: Who?

MARK: Menkes. *(Beat.)* Jesus. Irving Menkes—with the cauliflower nose.

MEYER: Menkes is dead.

MARK: When did he die?

MEYER: Five years. I don't know. Everyone's dead. He had a heart attack at a senior's dance.

MARK: I want you to go to therapy.

MEYER: Feh.

MARK: Don't feh. I paid for it.

MEYER: I heard a story once about a man with no arms. He lost them in the revolution and couldn't make a living, so he wandered from farm to farm where he dug up roots and vegetables with his face so that he could eat. One day an old woman finds him and says "Yvanovich, what are you stealing my roots for? I should have my husband come out and beat you." The man says. "Mama, I have no arms. They were cut off in the war. I can't work. If I don't eat, I'll die." The woman says, "What do you want to live for, your arms aren't going to grow back."

          Beat.

MARK: What's the point?

MEYER: The point? The one hand works good enough.

          Fade.

Scene 2

          RUZIKA chases MEYER in the apartment.

RUZIKA: Take your bath.

MEYER: I'll wash myself.

RUZIKA: You will pass out and crack your head.

MEYER: My head's already cracked, I let you in.

RUZIKA: Hajde. *(Come on.)*

MEYER: Please, watch a program, or better make a kugel.

RUZIKA: I have to do washing, supper. Don't make trouble

MEYER: I can't. You see that candle?

RUZIKA: Da.

MEYER: It's for my Laney. I keep one lit for her all the time. In memory. I promised her I'd never be intimate with another woman.

RUZIKA:	I will use a wash cloth. When I scrub, you don't get pleasure. Go! I bez tebe imam dosta brige! Polude cu zbog tebe! *(Naked! I got enough to worry about without you! You make me crazy!)*
MEYER:	Zol zein schtill. *(Be quiet.)* I got something I want you to mail. There's a stamp on it, put it in your purse.
RUZIKA:	*(She takes it.)* Jewish Agricultural Fund–Planting Centre. What is this?
MEYER:	It's a memorial for my late wife. Everyone needs trees. I'm happy to help.
RUZIKA:	You bath, I mail.
MEYER:	Ruzika, I took a bath last week.
RUZIKA:	You never take. Come on.
MEYER:	Let me take my own bath.
RUZIKA:	Ne. How will I know you're OK?
MEYER:	I'll sing. If I'm dead, I'll stop.
RUZIKA:	Ne. *(No.)*
MEYER:	I'll keep the door open a crack. If I drown, you'll hear the bubbles.
RUZIKA:	All the way.
MEYER:	Half.
RUZIKA:	Potpuno. *(All.)*
MEYER:	If you peek, I'll close it.
RUZIKA:	If I peek, I am crazy.
MEYER:	You'll mail the letter?
RUZIKA:	An old man helps a forest. What could be bad?
MEYER:	Thank you maidelah. *(Dear.)* You know, I like a little oil in the bath. My elbows.

RUZIKA: No oil, you slip.

MEYER: I won't slip. I just got a forty dollar bath mat. If I slip we can sue.

RUZIKA: Ne.

MEYER: Why did they send me such a witch?

RUZIKA: You done bad things in a past life. I go make water.

                 She goes. He opens a cupboard.

MEYER: Where did she… *(Shouting.)* Ruzika, where'd you put the schnapps?

RUZIKA: After bath, I make one drink. Before *The Price is Right*.

                 She returns.

MEYER: So where'd you hide it?

RUZIKA: Ah. Ovde *(Here.)*. You sneak a drink.

MEYER: Bite your tongue.

RUZIKA: This was full.

MEYER: Mansas *(Stories.)*.

RUZIKA: You steal some schnapps.

MEYER: I didn't steal nothing.

RUZIKA: You think I got no eyes? You steal. I can see. Shame. Go take your bath. And don't fall asleep. *(Beat.)*

MEYER: Are all Serbians like you? *(Beat.)*

RUZIKA: Yes.

                 Fade.

Scene 3

> *The apartment. MEYER wears a yarmulke, he has just lit a second Yahrzeit candle and finished a prayer.*

MEYER: Forty years she's gone. My Bubba raised five children through the revolution. In the forest running from the Bolsheviks. They had nothing. She would build a little fire with some twigs and make a soup from the birch bark, with the snow. They almost starved. But they met a Polack who did business near the border, Kaminsky. He sold them tickets for the boat. Stolen of course. You couldn't get tickets. Everyone wanted out. Cost my Bubba two thousand dollars. But she got them here. So I light for her because there's no one else to remember. *(Beat.)* You light one for me. God knows the other one won't. *(Beat.)* You hear from her?

MARK: I wrote you had a stroke. I think she moved.

MEYER: Not a word since your mother's funeral. You have brains, but her...

MARK: Don't.

MEYER: First the drugs, then the stealing, then she didn't come home...

MARK: Don't start.

MEYER: What?

MARK: I don't want to hear it. Put you both in a room, and you can tear each other's eyes out.

MEYER: If the apple is rotten, do you keep it in the basket? Buhbzu, you hungry? I got fish sticks.

MARK: No. I gotta go.

MEYER: You just got here.

MARK: I haven't even been home yet. I...I've got a lot to do.

MEYER: Never mind. Hey! We got a Bar Mitzvah invitation from Eli Wasserstein.

MARK: Who?

MEYER: Yankel's grandson.

MARK: Who?

MEYER: Yankel. The cutter who taught me to make suits in Montreal. I was a pisher, maybe seventeen.

MARK: Why's he inviting me?

MEYER: When you went to Israel with your Zionist youth group. I didn't have the money, I borrowed from Yankel.

MARK: So why's he inviting me?

MEYER: So now you can give the kid a gift.

MARK: I can't go to Montreal.

MEYER: Why not?

MARK: I have school.

MEYER: It's a Saturday. *(Beat.)* So we'll go.

MARK: You can't. You're sick.

MEYER: Loz mir uhp. *(Leave me be.)* We'll take the train.

MARK: You had a stroke Dad.

MEYER: I didn't die. I owe Yankel. It's an insult not to go.

MARK: I'll send a gift.

MEYER: I haven't been to Montreal, must be five years. And then for a funeral. We'll stay at Ruby Foos.

MARK: That's in the middle of nowhere.

MEYER: I want to visit my mother and father. It's near the cemetery. We can take a cab to the Main and get smoked meat.

MARK: You're not allowed that.

MEYER: From Schwartz's. A nice medium sandwich. French fries. A little speck on the side, some banana peppers, a cherry coke. And a pickle. That I could go for.

MARK: And drop dead on the spot.

MEYER: A juicy smoked meat. That would make me happy, the best medicine. Here. You got pishuchs. Dreck. That one by the O'Keefe The-Atre.

MARK: Shopsy's.

MEYER: Uch.

MARK: They make a decent sandwich.

MEYER: Please. Ich bin dir moichel Shopsy's. *(Please spare me Shopsy's.)* I had from them once a sandwich. Like sandpaper. They pile it high in front, in back there's nothing. The meat is cold, dry and tasteless. Mustard like it was rationed. I'd rather have pinworms than eat one of them. In Montreal you get a sandwich, juicy, nice. Here it's shleppers. Goyishe sandwiches. You used to walk down St. Lawrence boulevard and go to any kinda delicatessen. Lester's, Schwartz's, Levitz. They all smoked their own briskets. In my day you'd get a sandwich, a pickle and a Coca-Cola for a dime. A dime! I ate a lot of sandwiches in my time. Boy could I eat a sandwich from Schwartz's.

MARK: Well you won't be eating stuff like that any more.

MEYER: Then I'd be happy to die right now. I'm not going on that diet.

MARK: What diet?

MEYER: The no smoked meat diet. The train is comfortable. You get the tickets.

    Fade.

Scene 4

The apartment. MEYER is in the doorway with DEVON. DEVON is dressed as a boy scout.

MEYER: What do you want?

DEVON: Do you want to sponsor me for the Wolverine Bowlathon?

MEYER: The what?

DEVON: The Wolverine Bowlathon.

MEYER: What's that?

DEVON: Bowling to raise money for the Wolverines.

MEYER: Whatta you do with the money?

DEVON: Go to camp.

MEYER: Camp. What camp?

DEVON: Wolverine Camp.

MEYER: What's that?

DEVON: It's a camp.

MEYER: Like a concentration camp? You know what a concentration camp is?

DEVON: No.

MEYER: Never mind. Come in. I don't need the whole building to know my business.

DEVON: I'm not supposed to.

MEYER: You live downstairs?

DEVON: Ya.

MEYER: I'm gonna kidnap someone lives downstairs? You're making a draft. Come in.

He comes in.

	You want a candy?
DEVON:	No thank you.
MEYER:	It's chocolate. *(He offers the candy dish.)*
DEVON:	No thank you.
MEYER:	You don't want, dafminisht. *(Never mind.)* So how much for this bowlingthon?
DEVON:	Twenty cents a pin. If I get a strike, it's two dollars.
MEYER:	Two dollars! If you get ten strikes?
DEVON:	Twenty dollars.
MEYER:	Twenty dollars! Why should I give you twenty dollars?
DEVON:	You have to sponsor me first.
MEYER:	What do you know from bowling?
DEVON:	Nothing.
MEYER:	So why are you going?
DEVON:	It's part of the activities.
MEYER:	Activities. You get a badge for that?
DEVON:	Ya.
MEYER:	What's that one for?
DEVON:	Sewing.
MEYER:	They teach you to sew?
DEVON:	It's part of the activities.
MEYER:	Activities. All right. You got a paper?
DEVON:	Here.
MEYER:	What's your name?
DEVON:	Devon.

MEYER: What the hell kind of name is that? You go to
                school Devon?

DEVON: Ya.

MEYER: Good. Stay in school. Maybe you'll learn
                something. And don't get into anybody's car, you
                understand?

DEVON: Ya.

MEYER: All right, leave me the bowling papers, I'll have my
                lawyer take a look.

DEVON: I have to come back?

MEYER: Such a smart kid. Give me forty-eight hours, I don't
                like being rushed.

DEVON: OK.

MEYER: I'll tell you what. Someone's making a mess with
                pictures on the stoop. I see it from my window. You
                clean it up, I'll sponsor you. *(Beat.)*

DEVON: OK.

MEYER: We'll see about this camp. You clean up the mess.
                That's another activity. Good-bye.

                *DEVON exits. MEYER closes the door, sits down
                and sighs.*

                Fade.

Scene 5

                *The apartment. MEYER and RUZIKA. She holds a
                laundry basket.*

RUZIKA: Where are the sheets?

MEYER: You checked the hamper?

RUZIKA: Da.

MEYER: I'll find them later.

RUZIKA: You will wash them?

MEYER: I'm not a cripple.

RUZIKA: Since when?

MEYER: Sha. Why don't you vacuum something.

RUZIKA: I look under bed. *(She exits.)*

MEYER: Make some supper, I'm getting hungry. Don't look. Ruzika. What are you... Poo off meineh somins kep. *(I spit on my enemy's head.)* Leave it alone. I'll look after it. Please. Oy oy got.

RUZIKA: *(She enters.)* You have an accident.

MEYER: I'll wash it later.

RUZIKA: I'll put it in the machine.

MEYER: Leave it.

RUZIKA: Mr. Jacobs won't like that.

MEYER: My son don't need to know. Don't say nothing to Markie. Please maidelah.

RUZIKA: It's an accident.

MEYER: We're going to Montreal. Don't say anything. I'll call the agency and tell them how like from heaven you were sent. They'll put a gold star on your record. Think of your boys. *(Beat.)*

RUZIKA: You will call the agency?

MEYER: A girl like you is hard to get. They should know how valuable you are. *(Beat.)*

RUZIKA: I say nothing. You call agency.

MEYER: OK. Let me sit a minute, my legs hurt. *(He sits.)* So what do you hear from your kids?

RUZIKA: Go to school, stay with my sister. Good boys.

MEYER: Good children is a mechia. *(Pleasure.)* Believe me. I got one good, one bad.

RUZIKA: Why bad?

MEYER: Her mother's side of the family. Romanians. You know how you make a Romanian pot roast?

RUZIKA: No.

MEYER: First, you steal the pot roast.

RUZIKA: Then what?

MEYER: It's a joke.

RUZIKA: What joke?

MEYER: First you steal the pot roast.

RUZIKA: This is a joke, to steal?

MEYER: Never mind.

RUZIKA: I don't know to make pot roast. You know?

MEYER: No.

RUZIKA: So why are you asking me? *(Beat.)*

MEYER: Tell me, what's with the immigration?

RUZIKA: Ah! Boze. *(My God)* Ten times they ask "How are you going to sponsor your boys? Where is your money?" I tell them, I work two jobs. I will look after them. Still they want recommendations, statements, interviews. Because I am Serbian. My auntie sponsor me to come here, it take her three years. I can't wait so long.

MEYER: You don't see many Serbians. Usually an agency sends a black girl. My mother alla vashulum *(may she rest in peace)* had a girl from Barbados. Jeanette. Very nice. You're from where—Sarajevo? Kosovo?

RUZIKA: Zvornik. You know?

MEYER: No.

RUZIKA: On the border with Bosnia-Herzegovina. My mother—Pokoj joj dusi *(God save her)* come from

Smederevo, Serbia my father from Tuzla, Bosnia. They meet in middle. So I am from Zvornik.

MEYER: Zvornik Shmornik. What's the difference, I don't need directions. I'm not going nowhere but six feet under.

RUZIKA: You go to Montreal. *(Beat.)*

MEYER: I grew up there you know. Long time ago. When Napoleon wore short pants. In the Jewish neighbourhood. Jewish kids. Jewish stores. Immigrants. Like you. Poor people. Struggling. My parents came From Minsk. You know Minsk?

RUZIKA: Ne.

MEYER: It's next to Pinsk. Then they were in Odessa during the revolution. After they came to Canada. He made hats, she raised a family. Me. My brothers Jackie, Aaron, Maxie, my sister Gittle. All gone.

RUZIKA: Petero dece. *(Five children.)* Five.

MEYER: I ask my Markie for one, I get bupkas.

RUZIKA: Sta je bupkas? *(What is bupkas?)*

MEYER: Zero. You know what's zero?

RUZIKA: Da.

MEYER: That's what I got. Who's going to carry the family name? What was it all for? I did everything for those kids. I always put them first. When things got bad we left Montreal so they could make a life here.

RUZIKA: Why?

MEYER: With those goddamn anti-Semites, you couldn't stay. One day everything is normal, the next the Separatists want their own country. Oy. The business that left that city. The Jews. It was another exodus. For what? It's still in the farkakta *(shitty)* country. So we came here, like you—for the kids.

RUZIKA: I want my family out before who knows what will happen again. Stupid men fight for land like in a sandbox. The hatred comes and everybody goes to war.

MEYER: Sure. You can't wait for things to get worse, you gotta take them into your own hands. Give the Separatists an army, you'll see what they become.

RUZIKA: I have seen. Now I am afraid for my sister. She must look after the children. She has no husband, no money, my mother is sick. Boze. To je strasno. *(My God, it's bad.)* Everyday I ask God for help.

MEYER: Your auntie can't help?

RUZIKA: Ne.

MEYER: It'll work out.

RUZIKA: Please, even Jesus can't come without a sponsor.

MEYER: Things have changed. We have to be careful.

RUZIKA: From Jesus?

MEYER: Not Jesus, but the other one.

RUZIKA: Who?

MEYER: The other ones. *(Whispering.)* Terrorists.

RUZIKA: From Serbia? No. Terrorists in Serbia get to run the government, they don't come here?

MEYER: Listen, when you're Jewish, there's a terrorist somewhere.

RUZIKA: I knew a Jewish man, in Zvornik. His family had been there four hundred years. Gentle like a flower. He was beaten to death by Chetniks.

MEYER: Because he was Jew.

RUZIKA: No. They thought he was a Muslim.

        Fade.

Scene 6

> *DEVON is drawing an airplane on the wall outside the apartment building. MARK walking by looks dishevelled and worse for wear.*

DEVON: Hey! Do you want to sponsor me for the Wolverine Bowlathon?

MARK: What?

DEVON: Do you want to sponsor me for the Wolverine Bowlathon?

MARK: I was a Wolverine.

DEVON: Do you want to?

MARK: You got a form?

DEVON: I can't get it now. My mom is sleeping.

MARK: Oh. Well, drop it at apartment ten, I'll sign it.

DEVON: OK.

> *MARK starts to go, then:*

MARK: Hey. Do you want to be an artist when you grow up?

DEVON: No. I want to be a lawyer.

MARK: A lawyer?

DEVON: Lawyers are rich.

MARK: Ya, but they get rich off other people's suffering.

DEVON: So? *(Beat.)*

MARK: Never mind.

> *Fade.*

Scene 7

MEYER's apartment. MEYER is on the phone.

MEYER: Two hundred fifty thousand dollars, but in rubles, Russian money. You understand? He leaves the bank. Goes down to the river and the police are chasing him. So he throws the money in the river. The police find him, search the area, no money. They let him go. My great grandfather, Moishe was a fisherman. A religious man—mincha, ma'ariv, *(morning/evening service)* you name it. So he's out fishing. He snags a bag, reels it in. What's inside? The stolen money of course. What does he do? He takes it to the police. What do they do? They arrest him as a suspect. Two weeks he spends in jail, then goes home to wander the ocean with a net... The point? Genius. The point is I paid for the bath mat and you're saying I stole it... What are you talking...? I sent a cheque... Two months ago. What do you mean am I sure. I pay my bills. I sent. I don't give a goddamn... I don't have to swear? Go to hell and shove that Hudson Bay card up your ass! That used to be a company, they built this country, now... Ya? I saw your men's department, fil mit mitziahs, *(all the wonderful things)* you got shmatas *(rags)*. You should be ashamed. I was a cutter twenty-three years and I wouldn't buy a suit from you if it was the biggest funeral on earth. You got junk. Chinese suits you got. I saw a suit made in Haiti. This was the Hudson Bay company, ya...ya. Fine, send me a bill. I paid already! Gayin d'rared with you. *(In the ground with you.)*

He hangs up. The door opens. MARK comes in.

MARK: What was that?

MEYER: Wrong number.

MARK: I heard yelling.

MEYER: He was deaf, I had to yell.

MARK: *(Looking around.)* Is Ruzika here?

MEYER: Who?

MARK: Ruzika. *(Beat.)* The Serbian.

MEYER: She went back.

MARK: What?

MEYER: To Serburbia. Her mother died. She went back.

MARK: When?

MEYER: A few days.

MARK: You shouldn't be alone all the time.

MEYER: Don't worry I got canned fish in the cupboard, I could live for fifty years. Did you get the tickets?

MARK: For what?

MEYER: Montreal.

MARK: No.

MEYER: What are you waiting for?

    Beat.

MARK: I have to talk to Carol.

MEYER: She can come too.

MARK: She can't.

MEYER: I never see her.

MARK: She's busy. She's a busy woman.

MEYER: Uh huh… Lawyers have babies too you know. That's where little lawyers come from.

    Beat.

MARK: We're splitting up.

MEYER: What?

MARK: We're not happy.

MEYER: You're man and wife, what does happiness got to do with it?

MARK: It's... Anyway that's it. Now you know.

MEYER: I'm never gonna see grandchildren? Buhbzu, get her pregnant. Children bind you together.

MARK: It's finished.

MEYER: The Jacob name dies with you? Why are you splitting?

MARK: I told you.

MEYER: Please. No one breaks up, something breaks them.

MARK: No, she... She had an affair. With some lawyer. Some... Anyway, I want to change things too. Shake things up.

MEYER: In my day, you wanted to shake things up, you sat in a chair until the feeling passed. Markie. Make it up. Forgive her.

MARK: Dad.

MEYER: I'm telling you.

MARK: It's not...

MEYER: Everything happens to my kids.

MARK: It happened to you too.

MEYER: I had a family already. You're mother went crazy with the menopause and threw me out, I was a man almost sixty. I did my duty.

(Beat.) What are you eating, you look like you came from Auschwitz. You want Chinese?

MARK: No.

MEYER: Your wife goes meshuggah *(crazy)*, you still have to eat.

MARK: I do.

MEYER: Did you at least make an effort?

MARK: Yes.

MEYER: Women aren't like us you know, they want you to really try.

MARK: I know.

MEYER: You know. Your mother kicked me out after thirty-eight years. I thought we were happy, she knew better. You don't know. You don't make an effort, you don't get results.

MARK: Stop it.

MEYER: You hit it with a hammer you're gonna put a hole in it.

MARK: It's my business, I'll look after it.

MEYER: If you…

MARK: Goddamnit, leave it alone! God. It's over. Finished. I'm moving out, that's it.

            (*Beat.*) It's no good. That's all.

            (*Pause.*) I wanted to ask…

MEYER: What?

MARK: If I could stay, until I get a place. If it's a problem I could…

MEYER: What problem, stay Buhbzu. Sleep in the den.

MARK: It's just until…

MEYER: You're my son, I don't need explanations. Stay.

                   Fade.

Scene 8

> *The apartment. DEVON is filling out the bowling form and occasionally takes a candy from the dish. MEYER sits on the couch.*

MEYER: My age? Why do they need my age?

DEVON: I don't know, it says.

MEYER: The whole world needs to know how old I am? Thirty-seven.

DEVON: You're not thirty-seven.

MEYER: Who are you, the police? Fill it in.

DEVON: What's your profession?

MEYER: Super model.

DEVON: Your annual income?

MEYER: Whose business is that?

DEVON: It's for the profile.

MEYER: You want a profile? *(He shows the side of his face.)* There. That's my profile. How long's this going to take, I got a headache.

DEVON: Level of education?

MEYER: I have Ph.D. in mind your own business. Next.

DEVON: Are you married?

MEYER: Yes.

DEVON: Where's your wife?

MEYER: That's on the form? Next question.

DEVON: How much do you want to sponsor me?

MEYER: What did you say, twenty cents?

DEVON: You can do more.

MEYER: I already have to rob a bank. Twenty cents is enough. Next.

DEVON: You just have to sign.

MEYER: Give me the pen. *(He tries to stick the pen in his paralyzed hand.)* Goddamn hand.

DEVON: What's wrong with it?

MEYER: It doesn't work, that's what's wrong.

DEVON: How come it doesn't work?

MEYER: 'Cause God looked down and said Meyer Jacobs, your life is perfect, I'm gonna screw things up for you. *(He signs the form.)* There, take it.

              DEVON takes the form. MEYER rubs his wrist.

DEVON: Does it hurt?

MEYER: Sometimes.

DEVON: Will it ever work again?

MEYER: No.

DEVON: You mean never?

MEYER: I don't know. They got bionics now, maybe.

DEVON: What's bionics?

MEYER: They chop off your hand and put on a computer.

DEVON: They chop it off?

MEYER: Forget it. I used to cut a blazer and a pair of slacks in fifteen minutes with this hand, now it's ferklempt. *(Tightened up.) (Beat.)* I see you're still drawing pictures on the stoop.

DEVON: Ya, with chalk.

MEYER: What was that yesterday?

DEVON: An airplane.

MEYER: An airplane? I thought it was a chicken.

DEVON: No, an airplane.

MEYER: If you say so. Remind me never to fly with you. OK, Da Vinci, I gotta lie down. You got what you need?

DEVON: Ya.

MEYER: OK. You bowl a perfect game you're gonna bankrupt me. Throw a few in the gutter.

                Fade.

Scene 9

                The apartment. Evening. MARK is dressed from work and is bringing some food to the table. MEYER stands over six burning Yahrzeit candles.

MEYER: Oy, do I miss her. Never was a lady like my Laney. She used to make me laugh. Boy we had good times... *(He goes to the table and opens a photo album.)* Three years to the day. Time goes faster when you're dead.

MARK: Why do you have six candles?

MEYER: Five for your mother, one for the Yugoslav's mother.

MARK: Why five?

MEYER: If one candle is a blessing, five is five times.

MARK: It doesn't work that way.

MEYER: You know what pleases God? It doesn't cost more, it's the same match. *(Beat.)* You hear from your sister?

MARK: No.

MEYER: What's this, eggs for supper?

MARK: That's what was in the fridge.

MEYER: You saw the news? A bombing in Jerusalem. Twelve dead. Half of them were kids. Ah. They'll never make peace. *(Beat.)* Did you hear from Jackie?

MARK: I just told you no.

    Beat.

MEYER: I remember. Sometimes I forget. Get me some salt.

MARK: You're not allowed.

MEYER: Not allowed. Listen, when the time comes I don't want no machines. No artificial nothing, you understand. I'll go to my maker without wires. Give me some salt.

MARK: You do what the doctor said...

MEYER: Please.

MARK: With the pills you're on, Doctor Freid said...

MEYER: You know, I always thought I'd die a young man.

MARK: Why?

MEYER: I don't know. God snaps his fingers, you're six feet under. I'm glad Laney went first, it's no good to be alone.

MARK: She divorced you Dad.

MEYER: A divorce is a piece of paper. In her heart she was still my wife. Did she call you in the middle of the night crying— "Meyer, I made a mistake. Money means nothing. At least you were a loving husband." I have postcards when she went to Israel. "How I miss you. We should be sharing these treasures. The land of our people." Eh. My punishment is to be alone. *(Beat.)* Buhbzu, fix it up with Carol.

MARK: There's nothing to fix. Eat.

    Beat.

MEYER: My father once told me a story, which you
              shouldn't repeat, but a woman, a widow-Schafetz,
              Hildie Schafetz, her husband died from an
              aneurysm. One day a healthy man in the meat
              business, they were very well to do, the next,
              boom! He drops dead on the abattoir floor. They
              found him with his nose chewed off by a cow. A
              hundred dollars to reconstruct his face for the
              funeral. Nu, so he drops dead, nose chewed off.
              Schafetz the widow is hysterical.

              Your grandfather used to play pinochle with the
              husband before he died, so he knew the widow. So
              they have the funeral, go to the Shiva house, your
              grandfather gets drunk, stays late, everyone goes
              and the widow seduces him.The day of her
              husband's funeral. She must have been in shock.
              It's forbidden you know to have sex while
              mourning, but that's what happened. And him. He
              was a Casanova from the old days, your Zeida. So.
              Schafetz starts calling the house, wanting Zeida to
              come visit her all the time. So it goes on for awhile
              but your Bubbie's getting suspicious, why Schafetz
              wants him to visit after the Shiva's finished. He
              says she's crazy since her Morrie died. That was his
              name—Morrie! She's crazy and alone. She needs
              someone to go to the pharmacy now and then. But
              your Bubbie's no fool and she tells your Zeida, "I
              know what's going on, put a stop to it now and
              we'll make like it never happened." He says OK,
              but the calls continue. Then, one day the phone
              calls stop. Two days, three days. Then there's a
              story in the *Montreal Star*, how this widow,
              Schafetz, was found in bed with her throat slit with
              a butcher knife.

MARK: Oh my God.

MEYER: It was a big investigation. All over the papers.

MARK: Do you think he did it?

MEYER: Who?

MARK: Your father.

MEYER: My father? He couldn't eat a steak if it was a little pink, he'd cut someone's throat?

MARK: So who did it?

MEYER: You miss the point of the story.

MARK: What's the point?

MEYER: Your Zeida played around and your Bubba forgave him. Markie, make it up with Carol, have a baby.

MARK: Dad...

MEYER: I know what I'm talking about.

MARK: No you don't! We're not having a baby. God. She doesn't want me. OK. How thick is your skull? She's bored. She wants to change her life. Maybe this guy, maybe someone else. But not me. Believe me, I tried. I feel like an idiot. I don't need you sticking it down my throat, I'm already sick with it.

            Pause.

MEYER: Did you get the tickets?

MARK: I'm not going.

MEYER: What are you talking...

MARK: I'm telling you.

MEYER: You're going to send me alone? What if I die on the train?

MARK: They'll throw your corpse off.

MEYER: In Belleville? You want I should rot in Belleville? We'll have a nice time. Maybe you'll meet a Jewish girl this time.

MARK: I'm not going.

MEYER: Listen, Buhbzu, life is precious. Like seeds, or a gasp of air. You take it for granted but living is something you gotta do everyday. Don't turn your nose up at an invitation. You want to change things, live a little. Markie, alright, I wasn't the best husband. I was no good with money. I drank a little. I gambled once in awhile. I stayed at the schvitz a night or two. I turned your sister against me. But my plan all along was to enjoy life. I have no regrets. The bad things take care of themselves. I was in charge of the entertainment. Ask me how old I feel. Ask me.

MARK: How old do you feel?

MEYER: Thirty-seven. I've felt thirty-seven the past thirty years. I look in the mirror, it catches me off guard, the old man looking back. I was strong. Slim. Nicely groomed. Now I have to catch my breath on the stairs. Keep a nitro spray in the bathroom. Thirty-seven years old and sick like an old man. I see you, young, handsome. Mark. You're my son. I love you more than life. I wish for you only goodness and light. Trust an old man. Give yourself some pleasure. Come to Montreal. *(Beat.)*

MARK: I'm going out.

MARK leaves. MEYER sits there. Then gets up, goes to the kitchen and gets some salt. Puts it on his eggs and eats.

Fade.

Scene 10

That evening. MARK is unpacking a suitcase. He sighs. Rubs his face. Takes a swig of beer and sits on the couch.

MARK: Aie yie yie.

There is a knock at the front door. MARK answers it. JACKIE is there with a knapsack and suitcase.

JACKIE: Hey.

MARK: Hey.

JACKIE: I went by your place, Carol said…

MARK: Ya… Come in, come in.

> *She does. She puts her bags down. They stare.*

JACKIE: Do I get a hug?

> *They hug.*

MARK: What are you doing here?

JACKIE: Well, I got your letter about dad, and it's Mom's Yahrzeit so it seemed like a good time. I came up from Dallas.

MARK: Dallas?

JACKIE: Ya. *(Beat.)*

MARK: You want a beer?

JACKIE: I'm not drinking.

MARK: You?

JACKIE: Two years. I almost died.

MARK: What?

> *The bedroom door opens. MEYER enters in a bathrobe. He sees JACKIE.*

JACKIE: Hi Daddy. *(Pause.)*

MEYER: You're too thin. *(Beat.)*

JACKIE: How are you?

MEYER: Fine. So?

JACKIE: So.

MEYER: What kinda trouble are you in?

JACKIE: I'm not in any trouble.

MEYER: Please!

MARK: Dad.

MEYER: I'm asking a question.

JACKIE: I wanted to see you.

MEYER: I have no money.

JACKIE: I didn't ask for any.

MEYER: You spent the last you had on a bus? Or you hitch-hiked with the perverts and killers?

MARK: Dad.

JACKIE: I took the bus.

MEYER: From?

JACKIE: Dallas.

MEYER: Yenerek velt Dallas *(the other side of the world)*. You're a cowboy now?

JACKIE: I was staying with a friend.

MEYER: Not a man God-forbid.

        Beat.

JACKIE: I hear you had a stroke.

MEYER: I had supper too, now it's finished. Markie. Shopper's has a special on Q-Tips. Go down, get me six boxes. I need Yahrzeit candles too.

        (To JACKIE.) Nice to see you. Thanks for stopping in.

        He goes back into his room and closes the door.

        Fade.

Scene 11

Later that night. MARK and JACKIE are drinking. A few beer bottles are scattered around. They are inebriated.

JACKIE: And in Peru, I took mushrooms with this guy, Alejandro. He was one of these mystics I was hanging with and we were at Paca Lake camping and the birds were incredible; macaws and parakeets and this rain forest, the trees were hundreds of years old and they converged like a cathedral, you know, so beautiful. So we're on 'shrooms and Alejandro was standing on this rock looking over the lake, at the edge of the forest, and I was starting to peak, right, and out of nowhere this giant Ceiba leaf falls into my hands. Right into my hands. And I looked at it, how perfect it was, the ribs, the stem, the veins under the surface, the colour, the...how nature made it perfect. And for some reason here in Peru, in the hills, at the edge of this forest, by this lake at this exact moment in time, it fell into the hands of some hippie chick from Montreal. As if it had been waiting for me, you know. And I looked up at Alejandro, standing over the water, his poncho blowing in the wind, his hair on fire and I took a picture with my mind, you know. Clear as crystal in my mind, I'll never forget it.

Beat.

MARK: Mushrooms?

JACKIE: Whatever makes you happy, right? So, I camped a lot, sometimes stayed with people, sold bracelets. Guatemala was cool. Uhmm...I was in the jungle, did a G8 demonstration, took peyote with some circus clowns, got beat up in a disco, had great sex on the beach, got lost in Mexico City. Then I met this girl, Janice and she was from Dallas so I went out there... Mark, the desert. You've got to go. It's the most beautiful... The land stretches on forever. It was... What?

Beat.

MARK: Nothing.

JACKIE: What?

MARK: No...I just.

JACKIE: What?

MARK: You... You've done more in three years than... I
            don't know. I... I'm not who I wish I was, you
            know. All the things I was capable of, I didn't do
            them. I feel... It's like this break up is a punishment
            for betraying my dreams or... Carol fell in love
            with a painter, not a teacher, I can't blame her for
            changing her...

            (He begins to cry.) Everything's screwed up. Oh
            God. I'm so happy to see you.

                She hugs him.

            Of course I want you to stay.

                Fade.

Scene 12

                *The following morning. MARK and JACKIE still
                talking, now drinking coffee.*

JACKIE: I mean we were flirting, but I didn't take her
            seriously you know. Then we ended up on this roof
            top, full moon, the whole bit and we just talked
            and...I felt like myself for the first time in—I don't
            know how long—and... The sun came up and we
            went for breakfast and Janice paid and...she just
            makes me feel like I'm good, you know. A good
            person.

            (Beat.) Is that dumb?

MARK: No.

JACKIE: I never felt that before. I always felt like there was something wrong with me.

MARK: I remember when you did that ballet recital…

JACKIE: When I was nine? Ah, fat like a pumpkin.

MARK: After, you said you didn't want to go anymore.

JACKIE: The other girls didn't like me. It was horrible.

MARK: But you took that class for two more years.

JACKIE: I didn't care. I just wanted to dance.

MARK: See, I think you've been yourself longer than you think. *(Beat.)*

JACKIE: Janice said I should come. She said I'd regret it if I didn't.

MARK: She's probably right.

JACKIE: She said if things get tough, roll a joint, take a bath and remember you have a bus ticket. *(Beat.)*

MARK: I gotta get ready.

JACKIE: When are you back?

MARK: This evening. I have to meet Carol.

JACKIE: I was thinking of…

            The bedroom door opens. MEYER enters. Looks at JACKIE. Pause.

MEYER: You got coffee?

JACKIE: Ya.

MEYER: Give me.

            She prepares it.

MARK: Good morning.

            Silence. MEYER sits down at the table.

JACKIE: So where are you meeting Carol?

MARK: At her lawyer's. Across town.

MEYER: The lawyer she had the affair with?

MARK: No, the one presiding over the divorce.

MEYER: He told you his marriage is finished?

JACKIE: Yes.

MEYER: You didn't talk him out of it?

JACKIE: It's none of my business. *(She brings the coffee.)*

MEYER: Give me the Coffee Mate.

JACKIE: It's all chemicals.

MEYER: When I need an encyclopedia, I'll ask.

JACKIE: Anyone want toast?

MEYER: You got school?

MARK: Ya.

MEYER: You slept good?

MARK: Fine.

MEYER: You had breakfast?

MARK: Coffee.

MEYER: You're going to work with no breakfast?

JACKIE: Well, I'm making toast. *(She does.)*

MEYER: *(Whispered.)* You let her stay the night?

MARK: Yes.

MEYER: Without asking?

MARK: Dad, listen. I have to work and when I'm not
             working I have to find a place or I'm grading

papers. We don't know when Ruzika's coming back and in the meantime you need some help.

MEYER: I don't need help.

MARK: Jackie's here... She's willing to help look after you—for awhile. The rest of the time I'll be here.

MEYER: What?

MARK: As long as you get along.

MEYER: You had a discussion?

MARK: Yes.

MEYER: You want me to live with that?

MARK: What?

MEYER: She's gonna bring her girlfriends into my house!

JACKIE: God!

MARK: I don't think Jackie's going to do that.

MEYER: And the drugs?

JACKIE: Marijuana is considered medicinal Dad.

MEYER: I got piles, I don't take morphine.

MARK: I think it's fair to say no to drugs.

JACKIE: You know... Fine.

MEYER: She's not coming to Montreal.

MARK: That's three weeks away.

MEYER: I'm not leaving her here.

MARK: We'll figure it out. OK? We'll see how it goes. Is that fair? Dad?

MEYER: *(To JACKIE.)* Three years you turn your back on your family! You left your mother's Shiva, that's the last I saw.

JACKIE: Here we go.

MEYER: I didn't know if you were alive or dead. Nights I lie
             awake like a spider spinning stories of what's
             become of you. A prostitute, a drug addict, a
             criminal.

JACKIE: Oh please.

MEYER: What's the matter with you! You grew up in Cote
             St. Luc for Christ's sake!

JACKIE: I am so far from that person Daddy.

MEYER: I waited three years to see your face.

JACKIE: How were your travels, Jackie? What's Brazil like?

MEYER: Eh, you're the same dreck *(shit)* as when you ran
             away.

JACKIE: I didn't run away.

MEYER: Please. You ran off after your mother's funeral.

JACKIE: You've lost your mind.

MEYER: So why did you go?

JACKIE: This was a mistake.

MARK: Jackie. Jackie, where are you going?

JACKIE: I'm getting my stuff.

MARK: Sit down.

JACKIE: No.

MEYER: Let her go.

MARK: Jackie, don't.

JACKIE: You know, if you'd done something with your life
             you wouldn't be the bitter old man that you are.

MARK: Come on.

MEYER: I got what to be bitter at.

MARK: Dad, sit down.

MEYER: What for? To listen to her poison?

JACKIE: Any poison in me comes from you. Anything I did wrong, I learned from you.

MARK: Don't do this.

JACKIE: Mom left you, and I left, Mark's just the sucker who got stuck with you.

MARK: Please. Jackie. Please.

JACKIE: No wonder his life's in the toilet. Good work Dad.

MEYER: Why not buy a gun and shoot me.

> *Knock at the door.*

I'll get it.

> *MARK goes to answer it.*

I said I'll get it. An old man can still open a door.

> *MEYER answers it. DEVON is there dressed as a Wolverine.*

It's Davey Crockett.

DEVON: I came to collect for the bowlathon.

MEYER: How many strikes you get?

DEVON: None.

MEYER: Tough luck. What's the damage?

DEVON: Thirty-six dollars and sixty cents.

MEYER: You got proof?

> *DEVON shows his sheet.*

Alright. *(He grabs his left arm.)* Markie, give me some money, I didn't get to the bank.

He suddenly collapses onto the floor. Everyone goes still.

JACKIE: Oh my God.

MARK: Dad. Dad!

MARK is over the body trying to revive him. DEVON steps forward trying to see.

JACKIE: Oh my God. Mark!

MARK: Dad! Dad. *(He lightly slaps his face.)*

JACKIE: Daddy.

DEVON: He fell down.

MARK: Can you hear me? *(Listens for breath.)*

JACKIE: Is he breathing?

DEVON: He needs help.

MARK: Call 911.

JACKIE: What's the number?

MARK: 911! Dad? Jesus Christ. Dad! Get his spray in the…

DEVON: I can help.

MARK: Please Devon! In the bathroom get his nitro. Come on.

DEVON: One, two, three, four, five. One, two, three, four, five. One, two, three, four, five. One, two, three, four, five…

One, two, three, four, five. One, two, three, four, five One, two, three, four, five. One, two, three, four, five…

MARK: *(Over DEVON.)* Wake up! Come on! You're not going to die you bastard. Come on! DEVON, please! Jackie, did you get it?

JACKIE: What does it look like?

MARK: It's a spray.

JACKIE: What?

MARK: It's a little spray thing.

             Finally DEVON screams.

DEVON: Move away!

             *MARK, shocked, moves. DEVON goes to MEYER
             on the floor. He climbs onto the old man and begins
             performing CPR, counting up to five as he presses
             on his chest. He crawls off and performs mouth-to-
             mouth resuscitation, then returns to his chest,
             counting again. Lights go to black as they watch
             DEVON attempt to revive their father.*

             Fade.

             End of Act I.

Act II

Scene 1

> *The hospital. Three days later. MEYER in bed. IV tubes, monitor etc. RUZIKA stands there with flowers.*

MEYER: Look what they let in.

RUZIKA: I go away, you fall apart.

MEYER: You broke my heart when you left.

RUZIKA: Siromah. *(Poor man.)* How long are you here?

MEYER: What, three days? First intensive care, then here, I can't keep track. Look at me, like a radio with all these tubes.

RUZIKA: I make paprikash when you come home. Fix you up.

MEYER: I like it spicy.

RUZIKA: Burn your balls. Put the fire back.

MEYER: That fire's out. Now I light candles.

RUZIKA: I light candles too.

MEYER: I'm sorry about your mother. How was the funeral?

RUZIKA: She looked so small. There was nothing left. Diabetes.

MEYER: It's a killer.

RUZIKA: She is finished her medicine but never tells no one. Why didn't she say something?

MEYER: People have their reasons.

RUZIKA: Ne. You got to keep living.

MEYER: Oy maidelah, it's easier just to die.

RUZIKA: It's not so easy. It's up to God.

MEYER: Maybe I could strike a bargain.

RUZIKA: Don't talk budalestinu. *(Crazy.)* I look after you.

MEYER: I got my family to look after me, that's why I'm here. Oy oy oy. Kids. They get bigger but they never grow up. *(Beat.)* How are your boys?

RUZIKA: Moji divni decaci. *(My beautiful boys.)* Beautiful. They look like me, they must be beautiful, ne? Savo is tall as me. Bozidar learns to fix cars.

MEYER: That's wonderful.

RUZIKA: I lose ten years of worry to see them. But home is not home no more. It's someplace else. *(Beat.)* Sta se dogodilo *(What happened)*, Deda, why you have a heart attack?

MEYER: I'm an old man.

RUZIKA: My Deda *(Grandfather)* was ninety-six when he died.

MEYER: I don't have that long. I got a bad heart. It's generic. My mother had nine heart attacks. She lived on pills like a drug addict.

RUZIKA: You don't take no pills.

MEYER: I don't believe in it. When it's time, it's time.

RUZIKA: But pills can help.

MEYER: Let's change the subject.

RUZIKA: I bring you flowers.

MEYER: I thought you were going to propose.

RUZIKA: I cannot, you are not Orthodox.

MEYER: Jesus was Jewish.

RUZIKA: But he had a good job.

MEYER: He was a carpenter, I was a tailor, what's the
             difference? *(Beat.)* Did you check the mail?

RUZIKA: Ne. You need something?

MEYER: I'm waiting for a letter. I got a few more payments,
             I'm gonna have a little forest. For my Laney.

RUZIKA: You go visit this forest?

MEYER: They send a photo. I wouldn't go to Israel now,
             with all the troubles.

RUZIKA: You went before?

MEYER: Markie went. Laney was crazy for it. I wanted to
             send Jackie but she wanted to travel Europe. My
             family left Europe, she wants to go back. An
             adventure she called it. Oy. You try to do for your
             children and they… I would've liked to go. The
             Wailing Wall, the Dead Sea. I got a cousin there, if
             he's still alive, in Tel Aviv, Yakov.

RUZIKA: Maybe one day, you go.

MEYER: I can't go to the toilet, I'm gonna go to Israel?

RUZIKA: One day at a time Deda.

MEYER: Nu, so that's what I do. I can't read the future.

RUZIKA: Look it's four o'clock, *The Price is Right*.

MEYER: Ah.

RUZIKA: Bob Barker.

MEYER: He's an old man already. His face is like a freeway.
             Who wants prizes from an old man. That's what
             wills are for.

RUZIKA: Those prizes are really something, cars, vacations. I put you a pillow. *(She fixes a pillow behind him.)*

MEYER: Vacations? You don't need to go nowhere. You bring your boys here. I'll help you.

RUZIKA clutches his paralyzed hand.

I saw a program about that Yugoslav war. Cities destroyed. Millions of lives ruined. Genocide. Because they speak different languages? Please. One's this kind of Slav, one's that kind, what's the difference? Why can't people live in peace? At least make an effort. Look where we live. All the cultures of the world are here and we live in peace.

RUZIKA: My late husband's brother lost his farm during the war and was put into a Bosnian camp. He wasn't doing nothing, he was just in the wrong place. When he was released, he goes back to his farm and learns his wife and three daughters are raped and shot, and now a Muslim family is living in his house. He finds the man and tells him "This is my house, you must get out." The Muslim man starts to cry. He says, "My sons were killed by the Serbs, my house is gone. I must have a place for my wife and daughter. I am afraid to go home." Now my brother-in-law lives with these Muslims and together they make a family. So slowly like this it will happen...

MEYER sighs and closes his eyes. Beat.

I must go.

MEYER: Where are you running?

RUZIKA: To church. You sleep. I say prayers for you.

MEYER: In a church?

RUZIKA: Jesus loves Jewish people too. I ask him to give you a new heart. He'll fix you up.

MEYER: I'll take a little nap.

RUZIKA: OK Deda, you sleep.

MEYER: OK. Dovidenya.

MEYER closes his eyes. RUZIKA stands there as MEYER goes to sleep.

Fade.

Scene 2

The hospital. Four days later.

MEYER: I don't want to see no one!

MARK: It's been a week Dad.

MEYER: I didn't see her three years, let her wait. Check the silverware or we'll have Passover with plastic.

MARK: You're never going to speak to her again?

MEYER: Markie, she's my daughter and I love her, but she's no good.

MARK: Come on.

MEYER: She didn't steal right out of my pocket? She didn't drop out of school with the drugs? I wanted to send her to a trade school. I wanted her to go on kibbutz, she didn't want. She never did nothing with her life. I'm not going to let her kill me. I hope to God one day she'll straighten out, but some things, you can't fix.

MARK: You make an effort at least.

MEYER: It hurts me like you'll never know. What did I do to deserve such a daughter?

Pause.

MARK: I saw Bessie Schlumpsky in the emergency.

MEYER: She's having her face redone?

MARK: Her son's the minister at the interfaith chapel.

MEYER: The one that was in prison?

MARK:	Yeah. He's "reborn."
MEYER:	You know Solly's boy, Matt, the one who never brushed his teeth? He stole a car, went to jail. Now he drives a bus for Jews for Jesus for Christ's sake. Solly goes on picnics, with the ham sandwiches and the milkshakes. Feh. Seventy-five dollars I gave for his Bar Mitzvah. Plunk. Down the toilet. *(Beat.)* You gotta cancel the tickets?
MARK:	What tickets?
MEYER:	To Montreal.
MARK:	...Ya.
MEYER:	I wanted to see Yankel.
MARK:	It's two weeks yet, maybe you can go.
MEYER:	In a box I'll go. Ah. It's finished. You still send a gift.
MARK:	I will.
MEYER:	Don't embarrass me. You get a card with a Torah and some Hebrew.
MARK:	OK.
MEYER:	You got stamps?
MARK:	I'll get.
MEYER:	In my sock drawer.
MARK:	I'll get one.
MEYER:	I got. Why get, I got. *(Beat.)* You found an apartment?
MARK:	Still looking. *(Beat.)*
MEYER:	You and Carol... It's my fault.
MARK:	No it isn't.
MEYER:	Don't tell me. I know the pressure a family puts.

MARK:　　　　It has nothing to do with you.

MEYER:　　　Please. I know what's my fault. You get old, you learn to take the blame. You understand a little what life is. Listen Buhbzu, I'll tell you something you shouldn't forget.

MARK:　　　　Ya.

MEYER:　　　Come here. It's important. *(MARK approaches.)* Try to be happy. Things might not get any better. *(Beat.)*

MARK:　　　　That's it?

MEYER:　　　It's philosophy. Like an onion. You got to peel the skin to see inside.

MARK:　　　　An onion. That's my big inheritance?

MEYER:　　　Listen I don't got jewels and a million dollars but a piece of advice is free. Try to be happy.

MARK:　　　　Thanks.

MEYER:　　　Look at the mental kid in my building. He's got plenty to worry about and he's happy. Count yourself lucky, you at least can look after yourself. So, now you're a free man, live a little. Whatever makes you happy.

MARK:　　　　Right. *(Beat.)*

MEYER:　　　I wanted to be a heart surgeon you know.

MARK:　　　　What?

MEYER:　　　My mother wanted a doctor. From McGill. You could make real money, be a somebody, but my father wanted I should work for Uncle Eddie as a tailor. So it was a big to-do. They fought like cats and dogs. Nobody asked me what I thought. So my father prevailed of course and I learned to cut cloth. That's where I know Yankel. I measured pants, not blood pressure. Then, 1958 they went bankrupt. Eddie lost the business. The night they closed the shop on St. Catherine Street, my father cried like a baby. He thought he'd ruined my life. "You coulda been a brilliant surgeon." Later I started selling. For Gold's, Shreter's, The Hudson Bay. Everyone was importing, they didn't need cutters no more. "You coulda been a brilliant surgeon." I can still see him. He was a character. Oy. I think about him all the time now. What I wouldn't give to talk to him for five minutes. (*Pause.*) Tell your sister to go home.

Fade.

Scene 3

> *MEYER's house. Three days later. JACKIE and RUZIKA.*

RUZIKA: My mother went for pains in her legs, next- diabetes infection- she's dead.

JACKIE: That's terrible.

RUZIKA: Hospitals make people sick. I don't like them. You want some cookies?

JACKIE: No.

RUZIKA: I can't sit. With two boys, you never sit, here that's all you do.

JACKIE: What are their names?

RUZIKA: Savo and Bozidar.

JACKIE: Nice.

RUZIKA: You have no children?

JACKIE: None that I know of.

RUZIKA: Children make the world smile.

JACKIE: The earth can't sustain the population. Poverty is rising, water and arable land are shrinking. I couldn't imagine having kids.

RUZIKA: You don't have, then you don't know. I hope they come soon. I must go to church.

JACKIE: There's a chapel around the corner. *(Beat.)*

RUZIKA: I pray in Orthodox church.

JACKIE: Doesn't God hear every religion?

RUZIKA: Da. But he prefer Orthodox.

JACKIE: I haven't been to synagogue in like, twenty years…

RUZIKA: Why?

JACKIE: Because I don't think God exists. And if he did, I don't think he'd want women to sit in the balcony, or call them unclean when they menstruate. But it's also part of North American culture not to believe. Like Europe is way more religious than here, except we have the Baptists, who I don't get, but where you're from is pretty religious. Isn't it?

(Beat.) That must have been crazy, during the war. I could never figure out who was who. Which side were you?

RUZIKA: I live on the border. I am both sides.

JACKIE: Did you know people involved or…

RUZIKA: This is war, everyone is involved.

JACKIE: But the Serbs started it?

RUZIKA: This makes every Serb guilty?

JACKIE: No, I'm not accusing you of…

RUZIKA: Many of us are against this war.

JACKIE: OK, touchy subject.

RUZIKA: You think I am guilty of something?

JACKIE: No. No.

RUZIKA: Then don't ask stupid questions. "Which side." *(Beat.)*

JACKIE: Mark said they'd be here by four thirty, it's almost five.

RUZIKA: Your brother is good to look after your father.

JACKIE: Ya. It does him a world of good.

RUZIKA: You think good deeds count for nothing? No matter what God you have, good deeds is the way. Everyone do this, the world have peace.

JACKIE: Sometimes what you do counts for nothing.

RUZIKA: Sometimes. But family is the heart of everything, believe me. You find a place in the family, you find your place in the world.

JACKIE: But you're a million miles away vacuuming apartments in Toronto.

RUZIKA: I have two boys to raise. How can I do this with no money? Every penny I send to my sister! I have to support everyone from here! If I could be with them I would stay!

JACKIE: I was. I just— It's OK. Everything is OK.

RUZIKA: How do you know? You are a bird with no nest. You fly away. I have to make a home. You live in God's country. Here it's easy. You don't know nothing.

            There is a knock at the door.

            They're here.

            She opens the door. It's DEVON dressed as a Wolverine.

            Zdravo. *(Hello.)*

DEVON: Is Mr. Jacobs here?

RUZIKA: No.

DEVON: Oh.

RUZIKA: I can help?

DEVON: I wanted to see if he's OK.

RUZIKA: Very nice.

DEVON: And he owes me money.

RUZIKA: He come soon. Come in.

DEVON: I'm not supposed to.

RUZIKA: I have cookies from my country. You never had cookies like this.

DEVON: OK.

JACKIE: Hi.

DEVON: Hi.

RUZIKA: This boy saved your father?

JACKIE: Ya.

RUZIKA: What's your name?

DEVON: Devon.

RUZIKA: Devon, you're a hero. Where you learn that?

DEVON: Wolverines.

JACKIE: My brother was in the Wolverines. You go to camp?

DEVON: This summer.

JACKIE: That'll be fun.

DEVON: Ya.

RUZIKA: Sit. I get cookies. (*She exits. Pause.*)

JACKIE: So. How does it feel to save someone's life?

DEVON: OK.

RUZIKA: (*Off stage.*) You should be on a newspaper. Front page.

DEVON: *(Looking at the painting on the wall.)* Who painted that?

JACKIE: My brother. You like it?

DEVON: Ya.

RUZIKA: Here's cookies. Eat. I have more. You like?

DEVON: Mmm hmm.

RUZIKA: You save a man's life. Your mother and father must be proud.

DEVON: It's only Mom and me.

RUZIKA: Oh, that's too bad. I got two boys. They don't got no father too. When they come, maybe you be friends.

DEVON: Do they live here?

RUZIKA: No, in Serbia?

DEVON: Where's that?

RUZIKA: You know Croatia?

DEVON: No.

RUZIKA: You know where is Hungary?

DEVON: Hungry. That's a funny name.

RUZIKA: No, this is a country.

DEVON: A hungry country.

RUZIKA: Many countries is hungry. They only bomb the hungry ones. I make you Serbian food sometime, very good.

DEVON: I'm not from Hungary. But I get hungry.

RUZIKA: I make you kifle, fashir, sutliash.

DEVON: I don't think I like that.

RUZIKA: This is food of Serbia, very good.

DEVON: Don't you guys have hot dogs? *(The door opens and MARK and MEYER come in.)*

MEYER: I don't smell no paprikash.

RUZIKA: I thought something happen.

MEYER: What could happen? I'm too stubborn to kill. Look it's the Eagle Scout..You expecting me to drop dead again?

DEVON: I came for the bowlathon.

MEYER: I paid you.

DEVON: No.

MEYER: No? So call me a liar. Let me sit down.

MARK: Hi.

DEVON: I like your painting.

MARK: What?

DEVON: Your painting.

MARK: Thanks.

MEYER: You like that? I'll leave it to you in my will.

DEVON: OK.

MEYER: Oy oy oy, it's good to be home. Ruzika, the food in the hospital is worse than yours. No salt they tell me. How's a man to eat with no salt.

RUZIKA: Bad for the heart.

MEYER: You know what's bad for the heart? People saying what you can't have.

RUZIKA: I make you fish for supper.

MEYER: Fish?

RUZIKA: Fish is good for the heart.

MEYER: Feh.

JACKIE: Hi Daddy. Welcome home. *(Beat.)*

MEYER: So what do I owe for the bowling?

DEVON: Thirty-six, sixty.

MEYER: Where did you get such a cat's number?

DEVON: I knocked down one hundred and eighty three pins.

MEYER: So.

DEVON: Twenty cents a pin, times one eighty-three. makes thirty-six sixty.

MEYER: He's gonna be an accountant. You want to be an accountant when you grow up?

DEVON: No, I want to be an artist.

MEYER: Meshugannah artists. That's gonna pay the rent?

MARK: Leave him alone. I owe you thirty-six sixty also?

DEVON: Ya thirty-six sixty.

MARK: OK, thirty-six sixty times two?

DEVON: Seventy-three twenty.

MARK: OK, here's a hundred bucks.

DEVON: I don't have change.

MARK: You know what I saw? Down at Alistairs there's a special on sketch pads for twelve ninety-five. And you can get a box of pastels for about the same.

DEVON: What's pastels?

MARK: They're like oily crayons. They smudge good. Check it out.

DEVON: OK.

MEYER: Check in now and then. I could have heart attack any time.

DEVON: OK. I'm glad you didn't die Mr. Jacobs.

MEYER: Me too.

> *DEVON exits. To RUZIKA.*

> You know what's good for the heart, a little schnapps.

RUZIKA: I get for you.

MEYER: From now on, I'm going to remember to live a little. Get out. Embrace life.

RUZIKA: No more schnapps.

MEYER: What?

RUZIKA: It's empty.

MEYER: It was a full bottle. What happened? *(Beat.)* It didn't disappear.

JACKIE: I drank it.

MEYER: A whole bottle?

JACKIE: I guess so.

RUZIKA: There's some Mani-shov-itz.

MEYER: That's dreck.

MARK: I'll go down and get you a bottle.

MEYER: Never mind, I don't want.

> *He gets up to go to the bathroom, MARK tries to help him*

> Sit. I can manage. Markie, get a Yahrzeit candle, I gotta light for your mother.

JACKIE: Her Yahrzeit was two weeks ago.

MARK: He keeps one lit for her all the time.

JACKIE: Why?

MARK: It's what he does.

MEYER: What the hell is this? Jesus Christ.

             *MEYER comes out of the bathroom with two half
             burned Yahrzeit candles.*

             Who did such a thing? Look at this.

MARK: What is it?

MEYER: Yahrzeit candles on the edge of the bathtub.

MARK: It's nothing.

MEYER: What do you mean nothing, what are they doing in
             there?

RUZIKA: I saw them, but I don't know, so I leave it.

JACKIE: I used them. I took a bath and lit some candles, it's
             not a big deal.

MEYER: You took a bath? It's not for atmosphere, it's a
             religious observance.

JACKIE: I'm sorry.

MEYER: The shtunk has to take a bath with Yahrzeit
             candles? I need to see this? I should have died at
             the hospital.

RUZIKA: No. To be home is good.

MEYER: What home, this isn't my home. It's a drop-in
             centre.

JACKIE: God, I'm sorry. I screwed up. I'm sorry, I'm sorry,
             I'm sorry.

MEYER: You screwed up plenty.

MARK: OK, enough.

MEYER: What screw up are you going to do tomorrow?

JACKIE: I'm gonna kill myself, will that make you happy?

MEYER: Don't say such things.

JACKIE: Why? I can't do anything. What am I supposed to do, walk around like I don't exist?

MEYER: In my house...

JACKIE: I know, you're the king.

MEYER: That's right.

JACKIE: So throw me out.

MEYER: What for? Next week I'll be in a home anyway.

MARK: No one's putting you in a home.

MEYER: They put old people in homes.

RUZIKA: Everything be OK.

MEYER: With her? She doesn't have a pot to piss in. No job, no husband. She's gonna sell beads on Queen St.?

JACKIE: OK. I didn't come here for this.

MEYER: So why'd you come?

JACKIE: Because you were sick.

MEYER: I don't need sympathy. You ran away I made do.

JACKIE: I didn't run away! God.

MEYER: So why'd you go?

JACKIE: Because after Mom's funeral, I was in the kitchen with my girlfriend, Annie, preparing food and you came in, and said "It's a terrible thing that Annie's mother had raised a slut for a daughter". And then you turned to me and said if I had any respect, I'd send the Shiksa home and put on a dress. So I left.

MARK: His wife died. He was upset.

JACKIE: She was my mother!

MEYER: Then you should have stayed for her! A week you sit for your mother and *you* disappear. Where did Jackie go? She didn't even say hello. I was humiliated in front of everybody.

JACKIE: *(Interrupting him.)* I'm the one who did everything wrong. You're innocent and I'm the evil one. Tell me again how you never once raised your voice or hit your kids. How you knew the value of a dollar. How you were always a faithful husband. Meyer the Innocent. You didn't sit with my mother, crying about the mistakes she made. How she wanted a better life for her children. How she could've married a doctor who'd have been a good provider, You're lily white and I did everything wrong. I was a mistake. I'd be better off dead.

MEYER: You don't say that!

JACKIE: Why not?

MEYER: Because it hurts me! *(Beat.)* Because I love you!

            Silence.

JACKIE: If you love me, let me be who I am.

MEYER: I just want you to be happy.

JACKIE: I am happy.

MEYER: You're lost.

JACKIE: I'm not lost.

MEYER: So what are you? You're not a plumber or an architect. You're not a big shot in the bank.

JACKIE: I don't want to be those things, I just...I'm a...a wanderer, I wander from place to place, what's wrong with that?.

MEYER: Where did I go wrong?

JACKIE: It's not about you. It's me. I'm different than you. I wish you'd accept that. So I didn't make a professional of myself.

MEYER: You dropped out of school.

JACKIE: That's not a crime. There's other things to do. God, you come home and everyone wants to know what you've made of yourself.

MEYER:　　　So.

JACKIE:　　　So? I'm supposed to be an engineer? I'm supposed to be married? I'm the same person as when I left. I can't just change. I can't just be someone else. I'm me, that's it. That's what you get. *(Beat.)* Don't worry, I'm going back to Dallas. Tomorrow. *(Beat.)* Her name is Janice, Dad. She has long red hair and a Texas accent and when she laughs, her ears move. And she's a dyke. And she loves me.

MEYER:　　　Let her go to her goyishe lesbian. There's nothing I can do. She's lost.

JACKIE:　　　The universe has a place for us, we just have to find it.

MEYER:　　　I got a place, in the cemetery.

JACKIE:　　　*(She crosses to him.)* No Dad, a place inside. Where you accept things and move on with life. Where you make peace with the world and yourself.

　　　　　　　　They stand facing each other.

　　　　　　　　Fade.

Scene 4

　　　　　　　　The next day.

RUZIKA:　　　Come on, don't make trouble.

MEYER:　　　I'll wash with a sponge.

RUZIKA:　　　A sponge? I wash the sink with a sponge, you got to get in the water. Come on Deda, I won't chase you.

MEYER:　　　Good.

　　　　　　　　MARK enters the apartment.

RUZIKA:　　　Mr. Jacobs. Your father won't take a bath.

MEYER:　　　She's gonna push me under.

MARK:　　　You know how to swim.

MEYER: This is how you speak to your father?

RUZIKA: You're too grumpy. You should smile more.

MEYER: If I smile my teeth fall out.

MARK: I'll get some super glue.

MEYER: She got on the bus OK?

MARK: Yeah, fine

MEYER: Zie gesundt. *(Let her be healthy.)* As long as there's no terrorists on the bus.

MARK: I found a place to live.

MEYER: Where?

MARK: The east end.

MEYER: So far?

MARK: It's not far.

MEYER: What if I need something?

MARK: You get it yourself, you're not dead. *(Beat.)* Can I take my painting back?

MEYER: What?

MARK: The painting.

MEYER: You gave it to me.

MARK: You don't even like it.

MEYER: I don't have to, it's mine.

RUZIKA: *(Showing a photograph to MARK.)* Look Mr. Jacobs, my boys.

MARK: Very nice.

RUZIKA: Handsome no?

MEYER: They could be midgets from a Serbian circus.

RUZIKA: Go take your bath. Maybe wash out your head a little. Nice?

MARK: Very nice. *(He sees an open piece of mail on the table.)* What? Again?

MEYER: What?

MARK: The JAF.

MEYER: I don't know. Throw it away.

MARK: What's the matter with these people. *(He opens it and reads.)* It's a receipt for two hundred dollars. And here it says, "Total contribution sixteen hundred dollars."

MEYER: It's some advertisement.

MARK: Look.

MEYER: I don't have my glasses.

MARK: It's a receipt for trees.

MEYER: Again? They won't leave me alone.

MARK: No, listen. It's a receipt. Money was paid to plant them.

MEYER: I don't know.

MARK: It's in your name.

MEYER: So, I didn't sign nothing.

MARK: You didn't sign nothing? You've been buying trees in Israel.

MEYER: I told you, when your mother died.

MARK: That's three years ago. This is dated last month. And here. Contributions: two hundred every three months dating back to when she died. Where did you get the money?

MEYER: What?

MARK: To pay. Where are you getting the money?

MEYER: You're crazy.

MARK: I give you for rent, your pension is peanuts.

MEYER: I saved it.

MARK: From what?

MEYER: I saved it.

MARK: You spent two dollars for every dollar you earned your entire life. Now you're frugal?

MEYER: Ya.

MARK: Bull shit.

MEYER: Markie.

MARK: Tell me the truth! *(Beat.)*

MEYER: I saved on the medicine.

MARK: What?

MEYER: I don't buy it no more.

MARK: What! Are you crazy?

MEYER: Ah, leave me alone.

RUZIKA: He don't take no medicine.

MARK: How long haven't you taken your medicine?

MEYER: I never took it.

MARK: So you could buy trees?

MEYER: People need trees.

MARK: *(Stunned.)* You know, I thought it was my fault you got sick, letting Jackie stay here, and now... You never took your pills. You could have another stroke.

MEYER: So.

MARK: You could drop dead.

RUZIKA: Maybe he wants to die.

MEYER: When the time comes I'll be clean inside.

MARK: This game stops right now. I'm not giving you any more money. You understand?

MEYER: Don't be angry.

MARK: You're buying trees with my money. What do you think? You blamed Jackie for stealing and now you do the same thing yourself.

MEYER: I didn't steal nothing, you gave it to me.

MARK: For medicine. Not to piss away. You know for sure where the money's going? Who controls it? Look at what's going on there. A people who suffered so much, inflicting suffering on others. That costs money.

MEYER: You used to love Israel.

MARK: Dad. Israel isn't peanut fields and orange trees. It's not Golda Meir and Moshe Dayan. That's finished.

MEYER: I did it to honour your mother.

MARK: I light a candle on her Yahrzeit, that's how I honour her.

MEYER: She's gonna have a forest.

MARK: Dad, she's dead. You can't make up for the past.

MEYER: A place for birds and squirrels, Jewish squirrels.

MARK: No. No. No! What's wrong with you! You can't just walk all over me. Take my money, my beliefs and throw them in the garbage like they're nothing! (*Beat.*) I can't do this anymore. I can't look after you. I'm wasting my life worrying about everyone but myself. No wonder my life's in the toilet. Jackie was right, she couldn't grow here. That's why she left.

MEYER: Buhbzu.

MARK: Dad. You're on your own.

              MARK exits. Pause. MEYER looks at RUZIKA

RUZIKA: He's a man. He's got to make a life.

MEYER: I got nothing to leave. No grandchildren. No invention. Just some old suits I made. I wanted to leave something in his mother's name, which is my name and his name. And Jackie's. So the people there could one day look at a beautiful forest and know that the Jacobs of Toronto did something. *(Beat.)* What's going on there is terrible, I know, but Israel's a young country. Today, things are bad, but tomorrow-things will change. We Jews wandered the world without Israel for two thousand years. But God still wanted us to be a light to the nations. So. He's Israel. And so am I. It's for us to be a light too. If I plant a tree, one day an Arab and a Jew can sit and share the shade.

RUZIKA: So now you are paying for the future. All things have a price.

              Fade.

Scene 5

              Two weeks later. The painting is gone. A candle burns. We hear the sound of keys. The apartment door opens and DEVON walks in. He puts some mail down on the table. He goes back into the hallway.

DEVON: Deda, come on.

MEYER: I'm not Jesse Owens, give me a minute.

DEVON: Jesse who?

MEYER: The greatest athlete in the history of the world, you never heard of him?

They enter the apartment.

DEVON: No.

MEYER: He was a great black Olympian, don't you know
            your history? He made Hitler squirm like a worm
            he was so good.

            MEYER takes a blast of nitroglycerine spray.

            Enough history, get the cards.

            *DEVON opens a drawer and gets the cards. They
            sit down at the table.*

DEVON: Did Jesse Owens win a gold medal?

MEYER: He won four. He showed the Nazis they weren't so
            tough. Go to the library read a book. What are we
            playing?

DEVON: You only play gin.

MEYER: I'm testing you. Deal.

            DEVON starts to deal. Then noticing the wall.

DEVON: Where'd the painting go?

MEYER: My son the gonuf *(thief)* took it.

DEVON: Why?

MEYER: Are you dealing or talking.

DEVON: Why did he take it?

MEYER: He wanted it. When you make something, it's hard
            to give it up. *(Beat.)* Like your children.

DEVON: But it was yours?

MEYER: What are you a lawyer?

DEVON: No, I'm gonna be an athlete.

MEYER: An athlete?

DEVON: Like Jesse Owens.

MEYER: You got to train to be an athlete. Every day, your whole life.

DEVON: I know.

MEYER: So you know everything, what can I tell you. You shuffled these? *(Beat.)* Where's the Serburbian she should... Oh she has the meeting.

DEVON: Meeting for what?

MEYER: The sponsorship.

DEVON: Like for bowling?

MEYER: To bring her kids. I signed a form. Fix your cards.

DEVON: But you have kids.

MEYER: I made her a promise. *(Beat.)* Listen, I used to make suits for a fellow named Daniel Jackson. We called him Jack Daniels. A big Irishman, ugly like my feet, but the nicest guy when he wasn't drinking. So one day he comes into the shop and says, "Meyer lend me fifty dollars, I got a tip on a horse." I say "So, get it circumcised." He says it's a sure thing, we'll get rich. I say if I give you fifty dollars how am I going to get rich? He tells me he'll never forget the favour. So fifty dollars was nothing to sneeze at, but I go to the till and give him the money. Next day he comes in, orders two suits. Two thousand dollars he won. Comes the time the suits are ready, he doesn't show up. So I call him and say, "Jack, whatsa matter I got your suits ten days already." He tells me, he lost the money on another horse, now he can't afford the suits. So I say, "I gave you fifty dollars, you said you're gonna make me a rich man, now I got two giant-sized suits that no one's going to buy." He says, I'll pay you, I promise. So the business closes down, I never see the money. Ten years go by, twenty years go by. I'm at the physio centre for my therapy and who do I see but Jack Daniels with a new hip. An old man, you should see. Uglier than ever. He tells me this, that and the other thing and that he has a son, lives in

Ottawa, works for the immigration. I kibbitz him about the suits, I tell him about the Serburbian, he feels badly, naturally, says he'll call his son, see what he can do. Nu, they sent me a paper, I signed it, we'll see if it helps. So I tell you this so you understand. Even after twenty years it's not too late to make things right. You don't make an effort, you don't get results.

DEVON: Gin.

MEYER: Already? Are you cheating?

DEVON: No.

MEYER: OK, shuffle.

DEVON: You said you were going to give me Mark's painting.

MEYER: I got something else for you.

DEVON: What?

MEYER: Shuffle already. I'll be right back.

> *DEVON shuffles. MEYER goes to his bedroom and then comes back and gives him a B'nai Brith bowling shirt.*

DEVON: What's this?

MARK: It's a bowling shirt.

DEVON: You go bowling?

MARK: Sure. Before my stroke I bowled every Monday for forty years. This was my league. You can have it.

DEVON: How come?

MARK: You saved my life. It's fair payment.

DEVON: It looks too big.

MARK: Try it on. *(DEVON tries it on. It hardly fits.)* Perfect. You look like a mensch.

MEYER sits down.

You shuffled?

DEVON: Almost.

MEYER: Where'd you put the mail?

DEVON: It's right there.

MEYER: *(He looks through the mail while DEVON shuffles.)* Crap. More crap. Look a flyer for a shoemaker. You can have that. And... *(He stares at the envelope.)*

DEVON: What?

MEYER: The JAF.

DEVON: What's that?

MEYER: My Laney's forest. *(He opens the letter. There is a photograph.)* Das is mein fargenigen— *(This is my joy.)* Look at that. Look at that.

DEVON: It's a bunch of little trees.

MEYER: One day it's gonna be a bunch of big trees. That's a forest Devon. It's gonna be a beautiful wilderness.

DEVON: Not for a long time.

MEYER: What's your rush? There's plenty of time. Look at that. You see the plaque on the bottom there.

DEVON: Ya.

MEYER: What's it say?

DEVON: In memory of Laney Jacobs of Toronto.

MEYER: Laney Jacobs of Toronto.

He walks over and looks at the Yahrzeit candle.

Look Maidelah.

Shows photo.

DEVON: Are we playing cards or not? I have Wolverines at
              six o'clock.

MEYER: Hold your horses. I'm coming.

              He blows out the Yahrzeit candle.

              Blackout.